GAMBOLLING WITH THE DIVINE

Rienzi Crusz

We acknowledge the support of the Canada Council for the Arts
for our publishing program.
We also acknowledge support from the Ontario Arts Council.

Some of these poems first appeared in the following:
Ariel, Canadian Literature, Trace, Fiddlehead, Insurgent Rain, The Toronto Review

Cover design by Michael Crusz

National Library of Canada Cataloguing in Publication

Crusz, Rienzi
        Gambolling with the Divine / Rienzi Crusz

ISBN 1-894770-11-0

        I. Title.

PS3618.U88B73 2003   813'.6   C2003-902900-X

Printed in Canada by Coach House Printing

TSAR Publications
P. O. Box 6996, Station A
Toronto, Ontario M5W 1X7
Canada

www.tsarbooks.com

For my Father and Mother
who first spoke of the Divine

that's how I am…
an ordinary man lost in dreams,
searching constantly for God among the mists

ANTONIO MACHADO

These poems, with all their crudities, doubts and
confusions are written for the love of Man and in praise of
God, and I'd be a damn fool if they weren't

DYLAN THOMAS, *Collected Poems*

CONTENTS

—I—

I am both thieves
scrounging for the kingdom
and cursing the cross

JOHN SHEA

THE MAKER

balances things,
concocts me
for this world and the next:

on shoulders burnt under sun fire
he grows a head pitch as crow,
shapes arms
to thin sparrow bones,
has me walking with elephant feet.

I am crow
that lifts the last thimble of water
from the pitcher's belly
with heaps of pebble,
sparrow   free,
lightning-winged,
elephant smelling the deep slope,
catching gun sights in the wind.

And I am made
ready
for the Sahara,
with a black ugly beak
that knows there's water
trembling in the cactus

ready
for the small boy
practising war,
as he prowls the tall grass
with catapult and stones.

ready
for the white hunter
heavy with ivory dream,
as he strokes his elephant gun
and waits for the colour of dawn.

PROPHECY

When I was a child
and played my happy venial sins
with sunny abandon
in the backyard,
I said, one day, to Jack Jesus,
never, never again
will I touch the cookie jar
or steal the muffins hot,
and the rooster in the yard
searched my eye
and crowed loudly.

When I became an old man,
I collected my body
and the fleshpots of my youth
and withdrew
to the small cathedral of my soul
to light a candle to my darkness,
and in the flickering flame

I saw a shape on a cross
and it crowed again
agonizingly.

4

BEFORE-A PRAYER

Lord,

before I am born,
flood my amniotic sea with the colours of your world:

purulent wound, splattered blood,
giggling children on their hop-scotch bases;

those with canticles in their mouths,
cathedrals in their hearts,

those that host the screaming demons
in their hollow heads;

before I learn to laugh
let me learn how to cry,

that next to the sweet mango tree
grows the dark babul.

Before I exult, utter the "hooray" word,
let me in on failure's hanging rope,

the stabbing moment, the sepulchred meditation
on life and death.

Before I can dig into this curried feast,
let me hold out a tin cup on some busy street,

learn hunger's embracing gripe,
the utter coldness in the extremities.

Before I reach home sweet home,
detour me on the refugee's mapless journey,
his lost children,
the charred home he left behind;

before you show me death's harvest of white bones,
show me life in the joyous flight of the goshawk.

LET US NOW

"Let us now
in the embracing love of the Father,
wish each other
the Peace of Christ" so says Pastor Malone of St Michael's.

So, my brown hand stretches
to greet the old lady standing beside me.

She turns, glares, extends
a thin pale index finger.

I accept this one-fifth brotherhood,
still believing, still refusing to snuff out

the last candle to our darkness.

BEYOND THE CRUCIFIXION

Morning stalks
this sleeping room—
circles   breathes heavily
in the deepening light
as if to announce its presence.

Then when coffee and toast are done
it circles again, watching
my every muscle move, hovers
over my morning paper,
how I tie my black shoe laces.

Morning commute—
I sense some other in the car
craning its neck
to take in the CBC morning news.
I don't believe in ghosts
convinced that the world turns
on hefty illusions.

Somebody talked the other day
about guardian angels, their loving duties,
how they silently shadow our lives,
cling on to us like barnacles,
but without so much as a hint of their presence.
I believe in God
so the story smells of the Divine.

Or, consider this:
I think it's this God fellow again,
the Divine Magician, Trickster,
who stole into my bedroom at first light,
was at the breakfast table, the moving car.

7

Maybe He just cannot help himself,
takes his divine love so seriously,
is restless, concerned
about those staggering on earth like myself.
Maybe he wants to go beyond his Crucifixion,
continue the redemptive act
here and now and for ever.

Or, maybe he's watched
the sweet sand-box mischief
of his two-year-olds too long, too long.

Is there holy mischief in Divine surveillance?

"YES, IN OUR FATHER'S HOUSE
THERE ARE MANY MANSIONS"

Lord, say: Come
        I have a place for you,
I'd like to hear your voice
        and please, no archangel
Burning Bush, sudden revelation
        by the broken ankles of a fallen horse.

It's time, Lord, to redeem a promise.
        Your Blessed Mother once assured me
of the Kingdom of Heaven
        if I became a rosary nut!
I did so, and still recall the night
        I heard the wind bawl out,

the apple tree by my window
        convulse in pain,
some hand clamp shut
        the gates of hell,
the night I found my peace on earth.

I'm sure she understood my pain,
        saw my face grow beet dark
as mocking words found their target:
"Here he comes, fat rosary wimp,"
        or, "There he goes, Mr Santa Maria Rosary man,"

hobo who never knew
        the polished mother-of-pearl,
only cheap coloured glass,
        beads with crooked cross,
all so entangled,
        no fingers could quite unravel
the holy knots.

9

So, here I come, Lord,
    but before St Peter
stamps my passport,
    may I ask a few mundane favours?
I'd like my room to mirror
    my master bedroom
at 166 McGregor Cres., Waterloo.

A colour TV would be nice
    (preferably a 24-inch)
to look in on Colombo,
    Cosby, Matlock,
keep track of what's happening
    In The Heat of the Night.
I almost forgot,
    I'd also like to beg for space
for my kids, my good wife, Anne.
    So could you please increase the accommodation
to a small bungalow?

    If you don't mind
I was also thinking
    of bringing along
my ten books of poetry,
    some copies of the "Elegies" I wrote
for my dad, my ma,
and my brothers Hilary and Vernon.

I guess, Lord,
    all this might seem
very strange to you,
    but then again.
I know something of the Vision of God,
    the metaphysical state,
space without space, time
    with no name, legend or end,

but remember?
   I'm right now only in the prison
of my own shape, the heart
   the eyes still holding on
to thin glass, seeing
   and not seeing,

the flesh still breathing,
   heaving, the blood as the river
flowing, and yet
   I await Your call
that Heaven once promised,
   the one concerning
the small blue beads
   of my broken rosary.

SITTING ALONE IN THE HAPPY HOUR CAFÉ

and meeting civilization head on
with a doughnut, hot coffee, cigarette.
At the centre table,
suddenly thinking of horseshoes.
What if somebody mistakes me
for a target,
begins to practise his Western art?
Cigarette smoke snakes above my head,
makes a highway,
collapses.

I'm being watched.
Blue eyes suddenly a torment,
a torrent of waterfall,
beauty with a knife between his teeth.
So once again,
I must close my black eyes,
feel my legs climbing,
climbing
towards the sun.
Each crag, jutting root,
now a rung of mercy.

Lord, I must move, move
away from this darkness unasked for,
or make that second discovery
of fire: love
for the tall man with thrusting blue eyes
seeing nothing
but a blur of shadowed skin,
a spot on his morning sun.

SMALL MARTYRDOMS

Lord, let me pass
     the sackcloth and ashes, the body
that must be whipped
     for the skin to flower
like a bloody rose.

     Refuse the saffron robe,
the Capuchin cowl,
     those ancient fakirs
who would walk the fire, find God
     in some cold bare mountain cave.

Don't talk to me of martyrdom.
     Not with my low threshold of pain,
the fool in my head, that beldam hunch
     of the coward. Yes. Peter was impressive
in death, squinting at the Gates of Heaven
     from his upside-down bravado
on a Roman cross.

     So, settle for less?
Small martyrdoms
     from boredom's ugly progeny,
ordinary chores,
     common and necessary as breathing?

I mean dirty dishes,
     chapped hands, fingers
that would scour the pan's dark belly,
     wade daily through Sunlight foam
like some post-prandial penance.

I'm moved
from wall to wall, arching,
        turning, seeking the dark corners,
the vacuum's roar
        about my ears, an arthritic wince
invading my face.

        Come garbage day,
I'm balancing on the icy driveway,
        as the curb   waits
with civilization's broken toys,
        ichor and stink,
the Blue Box brimming
        with yesterday's news, Campbell's castaways,
Kellog boxes,
        flat as pancakes.

And when the snow drives down
        like monsoon rain,
listen to the crack of elbow
        as I strain at the snow-blower's starter cord.
No. I'm not smiling
        at the pain in my left clavicle,
the cold wind sneaking through my old parka,
sputter and smoke   snow blast
that never fails to find my freezing face.

HOURGLASS

You know me, Lord,
in the hourglass of my breathing.
I know you
in your words, your artifacts.

        You say, love,
and the face of God
weeps out of the mirror
as if I were a part of the nightmare;
so the Samaritan listened
to the cries in the havocking alley,
and I take
to the dank streets
with coffee for hands shaking
out of cardboard shacks.

        You say, hate,
and yes I see Lucifer
warming his hands
over a dank hellfire, screaming
for a sheaf of light
from the Seraphim world;
and I am at it again
planning my ugly menus
of revenge and hate,
how to spin the world
round my cynical dreams.

        You say, sing,
and violins coax in the waking light,
noon   the drums,
twilight   sweet serapina,
night   hot seraglio, lambada,

then utter sleep   silence.
How my world shuttles like a raven
between love, song and hate;
bird now magnificent scythe
agains the sun,
now mourning in chorus
for its dead,
then contradictory
as it fouls the siesta air,
or unfurls the skull and bones,
live meat dying in its adamant beak.

Who said the raven
is only shaped to a strident caw,
a sack of bones
without language or meaning or metaphor?
Who said the bird is beyond poetry,
the hourglass under God?

"…SEVENTY TIMES SEVEN"

Step aside, Lord
step aside—

This is my fight
      my blood to spill.
My back-biting neighbour has done it again,
      crossed the bloody line
when he pissed on my manicured hedge
      and prompted his Dobermans
to make my green, green lawn
      their toilet retreat under midnight darkness.

I can barely hold my tongue
when his fat wife
      harangues her two brats
in a decibel pitch that even a tuning fork
can hardly absorb.
I remember, though, one morning,
      hearing something very similar in the Pettah Fish market.
I can do nothing
      about those autumn gusts
that load his dead maple leaves on my backyard,
      choke up the birds' water fountain.
I can kill, though, with the bloodiest of thoughts.

Watch me. How I'll pummel his face,
      make red those pale sagging cheeks.

      I am ready
all pumped up like a champion
      for the mother of all neighbourhood brawls.

Damn!   Why now?

Forgive me, Lord, but your timing stinks
when you now show up your mantra of forgiveness
on your biblical screen:

"...Seventy times seven"

LORD, WE ARE LOUNGING IN THE PORCH SIPPING ICE-COLD LEMONADE

I can read these signatures—
your pale hollow cheeks,
how you slur your words, walk
your young feet
with the cruel arch of age;
your dark eyes, which once sizzled
like raven's wings in the morning sun,
now dim as the melting moon at daybreak.
That winter's day
when black ice grinned at your broken body...

How I would like to erase
your   pain,
let the joyous sun fever in,
a gentle blue rain
wash away
your sadness,
your collapsed waking days...

How would I argue your case,
try to unravel God's cruel mysteries,
re-tell your story with a happier end?

HE probably will look me squarely in the eye
and say through his scribe:
"not till the loom is silent
and the shuttles cease to fly
will I unroll the tapestry
and explain the reasons why."

But I myself
become the things I write,
an unabridged lexicon of pain.
I can only offer a lamp of hope
round your aching darkness,

try some telepathic wave,
if only to say: we are in the same rickety boat,
let's share the karma,
listen to the psalms,
enjoy the blistering afternoon,
with ice-cold lemonade in the porch.

A MORNING'S SEARCH FOR GOD

First, tried St Agnes at Waterloo—
comes the moment of truth
at Sunday Mass
when the pastor exhorts the faithful
to wish each other
the Peace of Christ—
and the old woman next to me
folds her hands on to her chest
and looks away   away.

Out in the parking lot,
I am reversing my car, and
a furred woman in stiletto heels,
gestures at me wildly, her right arm
flailing through the snowflakes—
swearing something   something
under her vapouring breath.
With God safely in his church,
she has probably returned to her own gospel
of colour and skin.

I am now walking into Zehrs Grocery Store,
when a young man, burly,
leathered like a Hell's Angel biker,
with his star-studded belt heaving
to his laboured panting,
accosts me brusquely,
to say:
        Sir, here's your wallet, you dropped it by your car!

THE SUN-MAN TAKES A TATTOO

At the TURTLE TATTOO SHOPPE,
the Sun-Man asks Donnae, the tattoo man,
to wound his brown skin in three places:
Lay it on good, Donnae,
and in flaming colour:
on my chest the Christ's head, my left,
a Valentine's heart,
cracked four ways,
my right, a baby laughing through a blue soother.

And what does it all mean?
asks the tattoo man.
Don't ask for answers,
ask for history, the pain
of my woundings, the diaspora
that runs through my life
like an alphabet.

And how do I nurse
these Christ-like wounds?
Keep these signatures for ever?
Remove the bandage in one hour.
If it sticks, soak it off, don't pull.
Bathe tattoos in cold water to remove dry blood.
Use only specified ointment. Apply lightly.
Extended soaking in hot water is not advised.
If scabbing occurs, do not scratch or pick.
Above all, keep the tattoos clean.

Christ! swears the Sun-Man,
and the crucified tattoo on his chest
winces again
like the Jesus of old.

GETTING TO KNOW YOU

In my green green days,
    life was mostly
        bananas and marbles,
and loving God
        & obeying his commandments,
were as simple as hugging my mother
    or listening to my father's gentle voice.

Then one April evening
   as shadows lengthened by twilight,
church bells tolled to incense & vespers,
    a priest   thundered
from the pulpit:
    the hammer of his fists
    proclaiming
    God's volcanic wrath,
    the eternal fires of hell   and those
    who will fry in them-
shuddering in my small skin
    I turned away from God's scowling face
wondering   all the way home
    about Divine love.

The robust years.

    "The dark night of the soul."
A lost father   a lost love   three aching children-
    a warm hand's on my shoulder,
    someone's leading me out of the land
    of scorpions and burning sands.
Faith trumps the wounded soul.

    Time ripens. Enlightens.

                The ways of God
gather light against the thundering darkness.
        I am, once again   loving   talking
                    to my God,
swearing, whining, or asking
            as a worrying child its loving mother,
and old lover his life-long love.

HOW I SMUGGLED GOD INTO MY HOME
ONE WINTER'S NIGHT

Of course, God can never be abducted.
No way would HE involuntarily leave
his heavenly mansion,
seraphim and cherubim,
beloved disciples, saints and cronies
and move into my modest bungalow
at 166 MacGregor Cres., Waterloo?

So, believe it, God was into this   scam
from the very beginning.
Wife, kids, neighbours, the mailman,
the Paper Boy, were to move and breathe
and have their being in blissful ignorance.
So long as I kept my mouth shut,
I was sure God would never spill the beans.

We tried the most proven modus operandi
in the business-disguise.
A knock on the door and the farmer from Drayton
walks in with his wife (secretly invited)
Reaching for the inside pocket of his leather jacket,

he comes up with a whimpering little lump
of golden brown hair, with ears drooping like earrings,
black-olive eyes flashing his father's
prize-winning pedigree.

So, into our lives,
the warm spaces of home,
into nooks and corners,
he loiters, romps about on his short thick legs,
for ever sniffing
the shapes of our   human artifacts,

and all the while
oozing innocence   unconditional love   loyalty
and   mischief
in nothing more than a wet nudging nose,
and a wagging tail.

Again, the Hour of the Unexpected!
when one February winter's night
the Divine took flesh once more
to show us how to love
and be loved.

Kundera, my friend, you once said that
"dogs were never expelled from Paradise"?
If you must know, I have one here
who voluntarily left Paradise for the sake of love.

PRAYER

One season, Lord, only one:
the white slope, skimming, skidding skis,
torches, stars, brandy in the hot chocolate;
for me, a demon spirit, pivot, speed,
a descent acrobatic, ether on my face,
for her, a smooth curving ride on angel thighs.

No sky with God's fiery head,
rotting fruit, no whirling of leaves,
the maple's stripping tease,
no birthing time, no green mould.

Give me only
the white slope, silent and waiting
for the new architecture of hooves,
the hot fog round my madcap mouth.

NEVER DISCUSS GOD WITH YOUR GRANDDAUGHTER

Talking about elephants,
how they could communicate with each other
though miles apart, a decibel range
way below the human ear,
my granddaughter interrupts:
Can an elephant turn itself into God?
Well, can he?
No,
but God can become an elephant,
is an elephant,
is *the* elephant.

Sure. Sure.
Then, my turtle, Happy, is God,
and so is Jen's black rabbit, Terminator.
Giggling, she turns
to bury her head in the couch,
and I cannot see the mischief
in her dark laughing eyes, only
sense the shards of my theology
digging into my sweating palms.

SPEAK TO ME

of how you hold your pain
        like a sacrament
in the tabernacle of your head,
        rein in those cutting words
like runaway horses
        without the crack of whips;

about the answer
        of your unclenched teeth,
unused knuckles,
        the dumb broken piano
of your voice, silence
        like a zigzag bolt of lightning.

Speak to me
        of that patience
that traps your welling tears
        and looks away, far away
as the clowning world, the damning words
        dance like imps
on your innocent head;

        how another's pariah deed
defines your compassion,
        an unfaithful woman, a havocking heart
fashions a mood   still
        as a dreaming pool.

Speak to me
        of ecstasy,
those fleeting moments
        when the world gently sways
in your hammock arms;

why you hold back the joyous word,
the clapping hands, the race's end;

so tell me
why the slow dance
        in your still dreaming eyes?
black butterflies
        pivoting like angels
in the maw of summer?

Speak to me
of that one great love,
        why you dance to no music,
whisper no sweet nothings,
        only let me imagine

the swish of your wrapping limbs,
        how the air bends
to your arching hot breath
        as laughter finally echoes
the thunder
        that rode your silent days.

Speak to me
of that God you say roams about
        the byways of your soul   shares
your loves, your barbeques, your slow walks in the Mall,
        those sunless days, those demon moments,

What, for Christ's sake, is the secret of it all?

THE PRESENCE OF GOD

O God, do something,
Your world is now wallowing in blood.
O God, here she comes!
God, how can you abandon me now?
God love you always, my son.
God forbid, if you should die before me.
For God's sake, keep your mouth shut.
My God, child, what have you done?
O God, not broccoli again?
God will get you for this some day.
God, damn it, the snow-blower refuses to start again.
O God, the devil made me do it.
O God, why the crooked road?
O God, why this God damn snow-storm?
O God, where's the land of eternal summers?
O God, I hate to say this,
but your timing sometimes stinks.
O God, take back the pain in my faltering leg.
O God, let not my poem die before it' born.
O God, this life is mine,
but hold my hand while I'm in it.

"Lamb of God, who takes away the sins of the world,
spare us, O Lord.
Lamb of God, who takes away the sins of the world,
graciously hears, O Lord.
Lamb of God, who takes away the sins of the world,
have mercy on us, O Lord."

THE BILIAN TREE

Lord, why of all trees
the Bilian tree?
Which once leaped into my eyes
from some botanical dictionary.
Ever since, it keeps moving in and out,
up and down my mind
like a yo-yo. Why?

It flashed again yesterday
as the sun quivered with blood,
then slipped into the horizon;
last year, when summer brought Mr McIver
down our sidewalk, his Shitzu
raised a thin leg
to my precious European Willow.

Why these images of appearance
and disappearance?
those moments that fashioned vulgarity
out of arrogance, a midget dog
thumbing its penis at my face?
And what's all the ducking and diving,
the lightning sleight of hand about?

Lord, the encyclopedia reveals
definitions, twisted shadows, shapes:
the Bilian tree spread like Batman
against the cinnabar of sun
belongs to the sorcerer,
whose fingers are crooked, black magical,
whose heart is imp, cinema,
Bilial.

No art of symmetry,
no Buddha, Bo-Tree Enlightenment,
no softness suggesting
a hint of godly love,
or water dancing over pebbles,

only a wood hard as nails,
where no beetle, silverfish
has ever passed
the corridors of flesh,
blood for ever smudging
the woodman's hands like a curse.

Lord, how could you?

AFTER THE SNOWFALL

Through garage-door lookouts,
winter hazed:

bleached bones   the catalpa
(without   its green crinoline head)

king maple   so humbled
frail white arms   skying

a tree
praying for its life

driveway   divided
snow walls   on either side

the Red Sea   parted again
and Moses   nowhere in sight

but Pharaoh   on his snowplough
continues history: walls the last exit,

laughs: there shall be no diaspora
today!

O Lord, mine are summer eyes-
tomorrow   the promised land?

your Egypt   still shimmers and shines
in its white   misery

THE CHATTERBOX LOVER

I love God, truly, though imperfectly.
But I have this trouble with understanding—
      God, prayer, his divine silence.
      Praying, I talk, talk, descend
      into this chatterbox mode, work my plaintive words
      expecting to hear the Divine voice,
      answer of small signs, miracles.

I hear nothing   nothing but the nothingness
of his silence, or,
is silence the thunder of his love,
the "godly" "no" to all my worldly desires?

If I'm not asking
I'm questioning   whining   cussing:

Lord,
      why the incurable stab of pain in my right knee,
      my sore back, tendonitis throb in my left arm,
      woman who fled my home for the dark night?
      My mortgage is killing me,
      taxes up,
      my goddam neighbour, his wild Dobermans,
      his overgrown privet fence!

Where I expect answers
      you give me nothing but
      a pitch dark silence,
      unsaid word, meaning what?

Lord,
      I think your description is SILENCE.
      My trouble, that I don't understand

what I don't hear, your language of divine silence.

So teach me
        teach me to listen, to keep my mouth shut,
        learn that when you say nothing,
        refuse small miracles, divine hints,
        you have already set in motion   currents
        of my next moments,
        mothering sea for my journey's end.

ELEGY FOR THE SUN-MAN'S FATHER

Father,
you were a great mathematician,
loved God and the jambu fruit.

You deserve a poem
exact as the sun,
with no beginning, no end,
just an intense line of light
curving to pure circle.

How can I, a child,
trace even a tangent
to your perfect geometries,
the vast afternoons of your brain
in which you walked so easily
with Euclid and Pythagoras?

And how can I compose
that mathematical prayer
of your living, the way

you chased the ultimate equation,
that something that flowed
from heaven to earth,
earth to heaven?

I'll compose
from the genius of my childhood,
use my crayons to draw the perfect tangent
straight to the tip of your tongue:
ah, the fruit of jambu!
How I shuddered and shook the tree,
and you and I
shared the sweet red pulp
of our mouth's yearnings.

FOR CLETA NORA MARCELLINA SERPANCHY

Dead and not dead,
gone and here,
you serve breakfast as usual:
hoppers and chicken curry,
coconut sambol, tea in the old pot.
Talking as you serve, questioning
as you move around the table:
have you brushed your teeth, child?
Washed your face? Done your homework?

Yes, yes, the answers mumble,
hoppers greater than truth,
half-done sums
no match for chicken curry or coconut sambol.

Yes, I grieve no more, grieve truly.
For grief is nothing without memory,
as love is nothing without the proven deed.
Night comes quickly by.
Your small hands lay out the straw mats,
three for your brood of eight;
nor do you forget the ritual
of hot milk and Ovaltine for nightcap,
and we close our restless day
with tongues on our saucers like hungry cats.

And how you shaped
the plum promise of Christmas:
Chinese crackers, bundles and bundles of them
tucked carefully in the almirah's bosom;
smell of French polish,
you on your knees squeezing out the shine
from veranda chairs, red cement floors,

a mirror to your sweating face;
and what about the milk-wine bottles
preaching their own sweet vapours?

I gaze once more at that one paragraph
with the deep scowl on your face.
You believing truly that rod and child
went together, love held deep
in your small fists. And your cure
for my brother Hilary's greed for soda pop?
Immersion theory: a case of pop, one rattan cane,
your hectoring presence,
until he could drink no more,
was duly exorcised.

And me, your immigrant child of the snows?
How in once foolish times
when all hope was gone
and the Afghan moneylender
loomed like a shadow of death
on my threshold,
you threw in the deeds to your house,
your money, your gentle voice of caution:
"Take care, child, take care."

All this
and how you loved the rose
with cow dung, bonemeal and crushed egg-shells;
the pomegranate tree
always so heavy with promise,
the shoe-flower hedge pruned to a prayer.

Mother, you are dead and not dead.
Gone and here: love, as the pappadams
crackle on your skillet again,

and you are shouting and chiding,
raving and ranting   loving,
praying, always praying.

ELEGY FOR AN ELDER BROTHER

After your death, Hilary,
I saw you flashing by in riding clothes,
a whip singing in the air,
boot catching the fire
of the sun.
Hunting? For what?
No quarry, no guns, no dogs,
only cloud and rain
about your ears,

and then I remembered,
I knew: the way
you held your eyes to Heaven,
ran your thin black fingers
over your scientific head
as the runnels of the heart
smoked and clogged
and you muttering the tried mantarams
of your life: Deus, Deus,
O Mother of God,
Thomas, my Doctor Angelicus,
Augustine, beloved sinner and saint,
Hopkins, Merton, Teilhard,
my wounded country, my Decima,
my dear ones…

Be still, O Hound of Heaven,
the helminthologist, the philosopher
is dead!
The worm, he always said, belongs to God,
is God,
his sweet obsession, his PhD piece
of candy, his metaphor for the good earth,
his perfect passport,
to the Academy of Acadmies.

WHEN TARZAN SHOOK HANDS WITH GOD

Many, many years later—
I understood the secret of Tarzan and his kingdom.

Herman Brix in the "New Adventure of Tarzan":
        a child watches with bulging eyes
        how the Ape-man fashions airy highways
        from jungle vine,
        saves Jane from the leaping lion
        with only a "shoo!" and a violent gesture;
        who bathes in limpid waters as crocodile snouts
        cruise a body length away;
        how by twilight he comes back to his tree-top home
        with a string of fish dangling from his waist,
        a basket of sun-ripe wood apple and mango.

Where paradise
        is eternal whispering of leaves,
        sweet mountain air,
        gigantic trees thrust their heads to heaven,
        poetry in bird song, mountain dew,

where the elephant comes like a hound dog
to his clarion call,
and God's silence seeps through
the waking forest like spring sap.

I think I now know
the secret of it all—
Tarzan's contract with God,
that warm handshake:

"So long as you refuse the sin of Adam,
so long as you see Me in every tree, shrub and flower,
in every creature that breathes and roams your kingdom,
you shall be lord of this jungle paradise,
Consider these as my favourite lines of poetry,
Learn them by rote."

DON'T ASK ME WHAT'S HAPPENING

Don't ask me
what's happening.

I wouldn't know.

Ask me
what happened,
had happened
and I'll teach you
how to conjugate life
in the perfect tense.
For I have loved,
forgiven, forgotten,
hated

with a white fire in my brain;
blessed, cursed,
laughed and wept
within these four walls.

Seen
the chambers of the heart,
heaven and hell,
here, here,
on this street,
this room, old church
tottering on incense
and candlelight.

I have known my God,
adored
when the world was candy and marbles,
questioned, beseeched,
when the dark clouds circled

like vultures.

So, only now am I ready
to let in
the happening thing,
that slice of time
that would dare to balance
on some gypsy's crystal ball,
dance for ever
in the camera's zooming eye.

My past,
those moments of time
I now hold
like a sacrament,
my tempered arguments of living,
epaulettes,
my bloody sword and shield.

THE DEN

Here, no fax or "surround sound,"
    IBM Notebook, fiddle of pop art,
or Beethoven reigning in alabaster.

Only "surround Lit.":
    great poets, novelists,
story tellers, philosophers;
    critics, with Frye and Aristotle up front.
Where lesser ones
    also bask in warm oak.

Where Goethe rubs shoulders with Ginsberg,
    Yevshuenko hugs Dickinson;
Neruda, Paz, Vallejo and Lorca,
    a huddle—
that's only Latin togetherness,
    ethnic solidarity-after all,
all these guys once danced in the sun,
    sang in the same idiom.

All the English boys
    circulate as at a cocktail party
(with a sign outside: BY INVITATION ONLY)
    For a moment there,
English decorum seems
    to have broken down
as Shakespeare spits on Byron
    and calls him a cad.
Byron gives him the finger.

Eliot, Yeats and Auden stand outside,
    grinding their teeth, talking shop.
Quite separate, Thomas and Hopkins

join Walcott, discuss rhythm,
plan some sort of poetic jam session.

As for Rushdie, Naipaul and Mistry
    and that whole breed of renegade eagles,
they are close to each other, to me,
    generous with advice, how to handle
the "bugger" words, fix the crooked line;
  Rabindranath (close by)
    has a word with Kahlil and says:
"Son, do your own thing,
    do your own thing!"

Something's going on
    in the Canadian VIP shelves:
Layton starts a wild
    argument with Atwood;
Maggie, far from tears,
    lunges for the old jugular.
Newlove, standing by,
    shakes his grey head,
takes notes.

Does "surround Lit."
    make a poet's den?
Stevens, say it again:
    "Poetry is not a literary thing."
What about the unexpected,
    contradictions of tempers, situations, artifacts,
sweetness, gore and God?
    Jungle theatre: the rose in the tiger's mouth,
how the tiny red ants
    take the bull elephant by the balls?

So, imagine this:
    I, born with original sin,
clone to the Biblical tax collector,
    Zaccheus of the sycamore tree,
sit comfortably among gods and saints:
    Dali's Christ looks down on me
through the ooze of his pain,
    and Mother and Child spew graces
through pale blue porcelain;
Joseph
    shows off his sacred family
in Italian terra cotta, Francis
    talks to the birds as Jude
waits patiently for my impossible days.
    The "IMITATION" lies open
on my desk, the Good Book
    close at hand.
Aquinas and Maritain, I know,
    lurk somewhere on these shelves.

Once again
    wisdom spills
from the mouths of babes,
    lays bare the den's true heart beat,
essential architecture:
my son walks in,
    looks around
and bluntly asks:

Dad, what's this,
a den or a church?

THE ALMOST FINISHED PRODUCT

Lord,
        is this it?
What you see,
is what you get?
A limping old man
with a plucked head of hair,

a belly full of age,
4 children,   a wife,
a mortgage, nine books of poetry,
an arthritic hip,
a memory thick as fog?

Where's the omnipotence,
your parade of perfections,
the 7 wonders of the world,
your cosmic geometries,
your compassion thick as honey?

Lord, am I one
of your rare mistakes?
Perhaps, a hint of compassion,
if you had spared
my black head,
a suggestion,
even a faint one, of a once handsome face,
would have been nice.

Why me? This dramatic metamorphosis
of flesh and bone,
this pain of seeing a happier prescription
for my eighty-year-old neighbour
swaggering about town
like some teenage fop.

The mirror in the bathroom
now stares back at me,
rolls its eyes and laughs.
Friends and neighbours are wondering:
"What the hell happened?":
the hallow cheeks, this drought of hair,
a waist line beyond repair,
the slow elephant amble.

Listen, my son,
"There is not creature so little and contemptible
as not to manifest the goodness of God,"
so you are in the kingdom of my goodness,
as much as the lowly earth worm, the snorting pig,
the reptile crawling on its belly.
If Heaven were cheap,
there would be less of hell on earth.
Look again at your omnipotent God,
how perfection seemed undone
by a man dying on a cross,
and tell me what you think
of the ways of the flesh,
and the ways of God.

BY SOMEWHERE NEAR TOMORROW

I'll be asking myself all over again
how will the story end?

I know
how it all began, I haven't a clue
how it will end.
The last breath must await the Divine chronicler.
Holding on to the story of the Divine
is like holding on to a beautiful fish
that slips through the clumsy fingers
of the hobbyist.

Without the faith, strong sure hands
of the sunburnt fisherman,
the kingdom of the sea will surely redeem its creatures.

So, Lord, you come in and move out,
as you please, well knowing
that I'm no monk, priest, or saint.
The way I look at it,
faltering souls need your love and care,
more so than Your beloved.
Each time I try to hold you
you bless and move away   away,
and happenings move in
like some sinister night.

Where were you
when the anaesthetist clamped his ether
over my mouth?
Recovering, you brought me flowers, a smile,
a blessing, but vanished
quick as you had come.
Why?

And where were you
when a restless mother abandoned our three small children
and took to the tea country with her lover?
It looked bad, Lord, really bad. Looked
as if you dumped me and the kids
in the valley of death with only the Psalms
to keep me company.
Where were your faithful commandos on earth,
your PR angels?

When at last you relented to my many genuflections,
the whimpering of children, a grown man's cry,
you come up
with the most unexpected solution—
You drag me out of the land of eternal summers
and gently plunk me and my forsaken brood
on a cold mound of snow.
Beware the unexpected hour, you once warned,
beware the face of disguise.

But again, you are the mysterious One,
Divine Magician
who from a mound of snow
would fashion another life,   a man of snow
warm as a Colombo sun, green
as the land he left behind.

LIBRA

The horoscope man
        looks at me   floating
under Libra's balancing star
        and says to my mother:

HM—

This one
        will surely embrace
the warming word,
        hear the lion
then quickly lie
        with the lamb.

He'll chase morning light
        as Apollo   Daphne,
refuse
        noon's obtrusive red face
wait
for the twilight hours,
        raven against a solferino sky,
to play his moods, his quiet poems
        of deliberation.

He'll walk with comfort
        among sinners and saints,
fashion love
        without tragic theater, touch life
like Beethoven   the keys
        under a haunting moon.

Yes. The poetic juices
        will run, but slowly and sweetly

like spring sap,
          and in the end,
he'll "go gently into that good night."

Wrong, my horoscope man.
          For three score years and five,
there's been no balance for me,
          nothing in between, no fireside poem
to lullaby the heart, only
          hammer and sword,
bloodstained epaulets
          on my tunic;
fire in a crystal glass, either
          the cobra's sac or a love
that would follow the Christ to Golgotha;

not for me
          morning's blue mist, only
the sun's tabernacle, the empire
          of high noon; no twilight
when the horizon hemorrhaged
          like a wound,
and the bird in flight darkened its wing
          too soon, too soon.

I took the dark night,
          with only the winking lamps
of firefly,
          solitude, poem, jungle theater
where the elephant   rumbled
          at his water hole,
the staccato squeal of water hog
          nothing more
than the boisterous order
          of life and death.

No.   I will not "go gently into that good night."
        You'll first hear
the Kandyan drums make fire
        under the dancer's anklet bells,
the raven caw the breaking news,
        the elephant's last clear trumpet—
and I, wearing the skull cap
        of the noonday sun, rosary in hand,
will seek the Kingdom of God,
        with the face of a sinner,
and the soul of a faltering saint.

—II—

But they wanted
to find Him
In their own way...
They would grope,
but they would find Him;
And gropingly
They did.

THOMAS MERTON

THE ACCEPTED ONE

For relics
     a black soutane
bronze cross
     lying limp
on breviary
     bloodied
with the martyrdom
       of celibacy

They found
     the cathedral of his cloister
empty
     Pray my brothers they cried
he now walks the earth
     without
surplice and soul

Father Magee opened
     a door
to the old cabook house
       a woman
and no icons
And God
     did not pitch the sun
with dark thoughts.

HANGING ON TO YOUR LEG ROOTS
LIKE THE GOOD EARTH

Raise your right arm.
Now grab a tuft of your hair,
try lifting yourself
off the ground. Impossible?

Think as God,
all things are possible,
some more than others.
Disregard gravity.
Both Satan and the Archangel
practised levitation,
not to mention the repertoire
of some of our stage magicians.

You might also have heard
how some holy men in India
read in total darkness, a strange light
spinning off their brains.

Still rooted to the ground?
Your legs growing heavier and heavier?
Would you now ignore
all this philosophy, history, experiment,
admit a power beyond your skin,
God in every hair, hanging on
to your leg roots
like the good earth?

GOD AMONG THE MALL-WALKERS

Slow   in a quaint arthritic style,
I've just managed to cover two rounds of the course—
Five is the conventional distance
for oiling the ageing bone, raising the heart rate,
and faking a smile at the roadrunners
who burn up the miles like a rich boy's Miata.

Forget the six and seven rounders,
I can only manage four.
Ankles now heavy as lead,
walking has turned to ambling,
as the leg muscles tighten and cry for help.
Forget about faking a smile
at the roadrunner showoffs,
in another life
I would have opted for a quick killing.

Lord, when did you come up with this idea
of a walking geriatric hospital?
Look at them: Mr McIver desperately trying
to pump up his heart
with five rounds of slow motion;
Maria Dupont seems to stumble every few feet,
the rumour being that her inner ear
is painfully unhappy.

Dennis Mumford, at 76+ attempts
to strut like a teenager despite the dire straits
of his prostrate gland;
and what of Sparky Cosmo?
He's the roadrunner with a crooked smile
on his face and osteoarthritis
in both legs. Sure, my roly-poly waist,

and staggering moves round the malls' corridors,
hardly improves the geriatric scene.

But, as if to fashion a fine balance, contradict
this parade of broken old men,
lovely young Maria Ponzanelli flashes by,
the Lord's happy therapy
of flopping blonde hair,
firm breasts, and swaggering buttocks,
for the blood-beat of those in the twilight
of their lives.

And Lord, how you cleverly shift the scene
from slow-moving old men on corridors,
to the Food Court turned Tim Horton's.
Gossip and laughter, the stock market blues,
terrorism, coffee and doughnuts, old men   retired   happy
with money bags jingling in their vaults;
their wives happily bunched together,
their mouths yapping as if time and coffee break
has no end.

THE CRUCIFIXION

(Salvador Dali 1951)

The Spaniard tries to reduce
all human bosh

to the slanting shape of a cross.
Fashions Christ's head as a gathering mop,

Covers our mad history
with a body perfect in its pain

from the moment we bit into the apple,
each time we sent our small world

rolling on its belly.
Look again. The pure light

behind the tousled head, over
the brooding shoulder blades,

a kind of effulgence,
the necessary fire.

As for the supreme peace below:
the fishermen, their beached boat and nets,

that's the other side
of the bloody equation.

GOD TALKS TRAVEL WITH A FIVE-YEAR-OLD SWEDISH BOMBSHELL

For Deena

Mission accomplished:
her last piece of Lego
sails right over the leather couch,
finds its mark in the fish tank.
Only then does she settle down
to God's simple question:
Deena, how do you go from place to place?
Fast in the idiom of the brat,
comes the answer:
with my legs, stupid!

Swearing something holy
under his breath, God gently protests:
No, my dear Deena,
what I meant was, how do you travel
from place to place, say, from home
to school, or from city to city,
country to country?

Oh! I'm sorry, why didn't you say so
in the first place?
Sometimes in daddy's Toyota,
sometimes in the big blue bus,
or, in a big plane
as when we went to visit grandpa in Canada.

OK. So that's all you know about travel?
Yes, but what do you expect?
I'm only five
and I cannot remember everything!

Of course, my dear,
let me tell you about
some other ways to travel:
on skis, ships (like the Love Boat)
trains, snowmobiles, dog sleighs,
horses donkeys, camels, elephants,
and even by whale belly like Jonah
who made it to Nineveh, or Habakuk
who got to Babylon in a jiffy
by angel wing.

God, God, are you listening?
or if you are hard of hearing
let me know, I can shout like my grandpa.
I have an idea:
since I'm so bored with Sundsvall,
can you book a trip for me
by whale belly to Waterloo, Canada?

But God just rolled his sacred eyes
and turned his face to Heaven,
leaving a little girl
to answer her own hard questions,
but not without his first catching
the sweet mischief
spilling out of her mouth like honey:

Mean old man,
        must have lost his tongue!

GOD AT THE POLO MATCH IN AFGHANISTAN

I thought I saw God at the polo match
                            looking away,
his silence rumbling like thunder
as far as the Hindu Kush Range.

Polo, the Afghanistan way—
                    No wooden mallet, no wooden ball,
                    no bourgeois horsemen
                    with honey in their throats, no
mounts
                    rigged and polished, tamed
                    to the lunge and the swerve.

A headless calf, still dripping blood,
                    dangles
by their fierce flanks as they scream, bucking
their horses, swerving, and lunging
for the final kill;
                  the sore ribs of their wild mounts,
dervishes with bloodshot eyes, playing,
playing with a tender life gone cold,
          a dangling trophy,
a bloodless crowd asking for more.

                  And once upon a time
                  a soft spring sun caught the first tender steps,
                      the romping,
                  the sweet in-between suckling time
                  of mother and calf in the open meadow,

                  and God singing with the red-breasted finches
                    in their brambled home.

HE WHO TALKS TO THE RAVEN

talks to God,
        black-feathered and -beaked
with toenails growing inward,
        a mouthful of caw.
Superb surveyor of the skies,
        postman to history
happening by the second,
        foul-mouthed, he sings
the sweetest gong, black-eyed
        he outdoes the morning sun.

He who talks to the raven
        shares parables,
some windows of possibility:
        if the water's at the bottom
of the pitcher,
        throws pebble after pebble
until the level rises like yeast
        to the top.
If the desert churns its thirst
        knows that there's water
breeding in the cactus.

He who talks to the raven
        talks to the bird humming
with ESP in its brain:
        who knows the distant agony
of the goat even as the anaconda
        unhinges its jaws;
the byways of the eagle's flight
        before it traps
the rabbit's frozen eyes.

He who talks to the raven
        long enough, learns
how sweet wood apple
        disappears in the elephant's mouth,
how to say: caw caw caw
        when gongs of hunger
ring like church bells.
        How when something lurches,
is ready to strike,
        can suddenly stride
into the face of the sun,
        keep the rose between his teeth
and say: caw caw caw.

This bird is bore
        and diplomat
will take your gifts
        and demand for more, insist
that you understand its importunate ways,
        love it, stroke its velvet wing.

When the raven talks,
        listen,
it is God
        in ultimate disguise.

THE SONG OF DAVID

(for Noel)

Night lies bereaved
of its stars,
dark timberline trees
pluck the wind's breath
for their sap.
Wearied men
with sweat on their stone faces
sit hunched, waiting
for the rustle of eaves,
or fireflies
to give the night   eyes.

When a gypsy boy sings,

and night cracks
to an angel's throat,
a golden horn in a cherub's hand,
weathercocks
flutter their wings and crow
and gargoyles laugh
from St Martin's dome.

A galaxy burgeons:
faces like burning stars,
their eyes and ears naked
to the sun
of David's midnight song.

And God opens a starry window,
gazes down
on a thousand hissing torches

burning night's pitch,
with David's song rising   rising
from a carnival of tambourines
and the dancing fire
of gypsy feet.

THE DIVINE EQUATION

Towards the end,
between spasms
of asthmatic breath,
father would talk

of God's fingerprints,
the *Divine Smudge*
the jaggery of human kindness,
Zaccheus of the sycamore tree,

and mathematically speaking,
of the Divine Equation.

For he
who gives back
the perfume of the rose,
its summer dalliance,
keeps only the thorn;

For he
who hugs the cripple on the street,
with his stump legs, gnarled hands,
empty cup,

sees nothing but God's exact sun
in his crooked shadow,
his squiggly lines burgeoning
to pure architecture;

who reads redemption
in the killing word,
and waits   patiently
for thunder to resolve
into a soft summer rain;

for he who's happy
in solitude, if solitude is his way,
but keeps his small ears open
to hear, perhaps,
the clink and clash
of rolling cat's eye glass,
God playing marbles
with Moses and Aaron.

Who chooses to pass
the lush green valleys,
for the high nightmare mountain,
and there slay his demons
of flesh and fear.

For he,
who'll be the one
to write the "embracing poem,"
show them what happens
on Monkey mountain,

how painted icons
like waxen wings

melt to the common colour
of blood;

the one
who'll fashion the raven's caw
canary sweet,
make the elephant walk
this Toronto boulevard in Perehara style.

GOD IS IN THE APPLE TURNOVER

Catechism class barely begins,
when freckled faced Angelo, the baker's son
jerks up his hand:
Teach, where is God?

Everywhere, Angelo, everywhere!
Even in the apple turnover,
right in the yummy filling!
But, Teach, why did He go there?
Won't all that goo suck him down?

No, Angelo, if God created the goo,
he also knows how to get out of it.
But since he especially likes apple turnover,
he enjoys his little dance
in the sweet gooey center.

And did you know,
that when your Frisbee wheels
and whirrs in the sky,
it's actually riding on God's hot breath
as he jogs invisibly close by?

Remember the wild clapping
that shook the cricket grounds,
the grin on the batsman's face?
Sure, it was the ball sailing over
the boundary line for a six.
But it was really God running away with the ball
to play by himself.

So, Angelo, God,
is always watching us
Right now, I'd bet,
He's counting the freckles on your face,
as you sneak into the house
with a small garden frog wiggling
in your pocket!

HEART OF THE MATTER

Where a door opens
        to the mood
        of your half-naked body,
        your knuckles still growing blue,
        a trace of blood
        round your mouth. Civilization
        with knuckle dusters on its fists.

Where a woman bends
        over a cradle, rocks it gently.
        And her song, her kingdom,
        is a lullaby in the air,
        her infant soon falling to sleep.

Where the reading lamp's yellow light
        picks out the still fierce eyes
        of an old man, a poem of hope:
        "Still falls the rain"
        Lightning round an ancient cross
        he had already seen, waiting
        for cock's crow and laughter.

Where the maid
        to this house of small rooms
        deserts her mop and crumpled beds,
        irreverent corners of dirt
        and stumbles into Thomas A Kempis
        all dressed up in sack cloth and ashes
        holding Heaven in a waterbead, singing:

        "Vanity of vanities,
        all is vanity
        save to love God
        and Him only to serve."

WHICH WAY?

A Bandit's Way to God 1

Mammale, my friend,

I'm somewhat confused at times;
things are moving too fast—
my feet seem slow
for karma's speeding treadmill;

when a man is nearly hit by lightning
more than once,
he knows not only the meaning of terror
but also how suddenly life can end.

I kill, but I am alive.
They bleed, but I am whole.
One moment a halo round a loaf of bread,
another, a midnight break-in,
crowbar in one hand,
somebody's blood crying out
on a cement floor.

What makes love and hate hold hands
in the corners of my mind?
Look at my karma's prescribed journey:
hope, the poor, the broken,
those who sleep with the rain,
who feel the Suddha's jackboot over their ribs.

What rage, what spill of blood, remains
in my troubled mind?
Where now that river
where Sirimale showed her mango breasts

through her soaking *idi redda*?
Menaka's tight behind
as she bent for the fallen coffee seeds?

Then midnight air, jungle darkness,
only mosquitoes about my tired flesh,
their thirsty buzz,
my cold haven of loneliness, fear,
a lone leopard prowling under a broken moon,
my own placards of death
scrawled in blood, the white hunter
waiting, waiting beyond the tree-line.

My brother, Peduru, shows me
his most recent sculpture of the dying Christ.
Talks of another way: salvation,
choices, forgiveness, redemption, love.
Nowhere the colour of blood
except on a loin-clothed God on a corss.

Over there, Mammale. Look at that forked road…

SOLILOQUY

A Bandit's Way to God 2

Ten more days, and I'll hold the dying Christ to his promise to
this good thief when the trapdoor opens and swallows my limp
body. This is the acceptable hour. To sit in this cold dark cell and
wake up from the nightmare dream of my life. These prison bars
that look in like windows to a life that has passed me by too
soon, too wildly. My galloping bandit days.

Dark nights of karma: the last cry of the Arab to his Allah,
before I laid out his bowels on the quarry's red floor; how small
were my victories, how high the price. Cruel, the deaths of Panis
Kapua, Van Haught, those others who got in my way. How the
aratchies threatened vengeance, shoved my father's head into an
unlit oven; Sirimale's unforgivable betrayal; and Menaka, whom I
lost; mother who never lost her unconditional and hopeless love
for her murderer son.

Now, the soul's journey from hell to Heaven. But before
heaven, Purgatory. Those dark spaces of doubt, memory, guilt,
regret.

"Why?" I'd ask myself.

Who'd believe the sincerity of my conversion? Can a man
change his whole life, redeem his soul in forty-five days?
How would my poor mother feel? I remember how she held my
small hand and took me to the temple for *bodhi-puja* and the
evening *bana*; her quick tug of my ears when I blew out some of
the oil-lamps at the foot of the bo-tree.

It's not funny now. When my little sister, Martha, protested
the torture of the garden lizard, she understood better the true
meaning of *ahimsa*. I wish I did. When my brother, Peduru, told
me the stories of the Christ, I yawned in contempt. I wish I hadn't.

No. I didn' t come to Christ on angels' wings. How my
soul closed its front door, fought back the intrusion. I told Rev.
Waldock, the Anabaptist chaplain to go to hell. The good Fr

Duffo often saw me in the worst of moods when I wouldn't listen to anything or anybody, not even my own broken voice. Nor did I come to Christ with an empty mind. I read the Bible, the small treatise on the virtues, the four last ends, which Fr Duffo had left in my cell. Brother Peduru's stories now made sense. The long, lonely hours in my jail cell threw open wide the doors of my heart, my mind. And I believed, listened to his voice: "He that follows me, walks not in darkness."

And so, the soul's journey to Heaven. Fr Duffo's Christ: love, forgiveness, redemption, peace. Not karma, but choice. Not blood, but love. Not darkness, but light. Not death at the end of a rope, but eternal ife.

I can imagine how the Suddha would laugh from their whisky bellies: "Sardiel accepts the religion of his masters. Ha! Ha!" How some would shake their heads and ask: "How could he forsake the religion of his birth? Forget the *bodhi-puja* days, the Vesak lamps of childhood? What cowardice is this from a man who once dared to defy an empire?" No. Not cowardice, but courage.

In these last days, I think I found at last what I had been searching for all my life: That mantra that would calm my rebellious mind. And yet, a rebel all my life, I go to my death still a rebel. For Christ.

THE ROAD TO DAMASCUS

A Bandit's Way to God 3

And Fr Duffo led me by the hand,
took me past my burning bandit days—

past Panis Kapua draining his lifeblood away
on a straw mat,
past the Nakoti Chettiar, his bowels
in his trembling hands,
past that dark smoking night
in the abandoned quarry
where the Arab and his magnificent Arabian
screamed and neighed for their lives,

past the madness of poor Van Haught's death,
past the fading footsteps of Sirimale's betrayal,
past the spiked boots of my white masters,
past the sucking sounds of the aratchies and their kind,
past the hell of my condemned soul,

to his God, the Christ
who waited all my cruel doubting days
to forgive all,
offer mercy for revenge,
love for hate,
Heaven for hell.

The one moment,
when "the Lord enticed me (with love)
and I was enticed,"
when I, Sardiel, Lord of Uttuwankande,
trickster, murderer, bandit for the poor,
found for the first time in my life,

love without borders,
love   despitemyself;
And Peduru's stories of the Christ retold,
the holy books under my red jail-cell eyes:
He who embraced the poor
with a love beyond measure,
"Blessed are the poor..."
Such music to my ears.

Another rebel, his against, hypocrisy,
the polished sepulchers of his time,
mine, the Suddhas with their jackboots on their huge feet,
their fat henchmen, the *mudalalis*, the *aratchies*;
his Judas to my Sirimale,
his crucifixion
to my hunted days,
my last manacled walk to the gallows.

But He, a God,
I, mere mortal,
He, innocent as a new-born calf,
I, guilty as hell.
I die for my sins, deservedly,
He died that I might find love at last,
hear his words again to the good thief:
"This day thou shalt be with me in paradise."

REMEMBERING THE "TALKIES"

(How to Fool a Pious Aunt)

1

Saturday afternoon. Teenage giggling and squealing. My two sisters Yvonne and Noeline having a great time with their close friends Queenie, Ziska, the Raymond girls. Before long, they decide to make it to the movies. Mum goes along with their plan, convinced that there's safety in numbers, the only condition being that they take Hilary or Noel as an escort. The girls usually select Noel. I sulk and often cry that I am out of this kind of escort service. Brother Vernon is totally immune to all this fuss about the "Talkies." His thing is pigeons, homing pigeons. Almost every Saturday, Yvonne and Noeline will lay this misery of their cinematic rituals on me. No wonder I am forced to take to lesser delights like marbles and used tram tickets.

2

Leave it to Hilary, however, to find some other creative way to make it to the "Talkies." He talks Aunty Ada into seeing a film on St Francis. She reluctantly parts with a quarter of her pension. Thank God I am included on this trip. We all arrive at the Regal Theatre fully armed with cones of peanuts, vadais, and small bottles of orange barley pop. No one is ever told that the film is San Francisco with Clake Gable and Jeanette Macdonald. Aunty Ada waits and waits for St Francis to appear with a couple of sparrows eating from the palm of his hand. He never shows up!

By the end of the movie, Aunty Ada is mad and squirming in her seat. She rises with noises short of swearing, shouts at us: "Never again. Never again!"

In one scene, when Clake Gable asks Jeanette Macdonald to lift her skirt to appraise the shape of her leg, I notice Aunty Ada close her eyes, reach for her rosary, and mutter something under her breath. It sounded like: "God, these bloody children." It just may be that the Earthquake scenes saved us from direr consequences; at least she refrains from spilling the beans to Mum.

THE GARDENER

Since Adam
had fouled things up
by trying to live under God
with a naked woman, a serpent,
and an apple tree,
this gardener's ambition
was to remake Eden
in only a garden of roses.

He would tell the story
of his labours
through lean dark years
in the grief of scars
on his thick knuckles,
his calloused palms
where dirt had churned
the beginnings of flowers.

When God's hot breath
finally broke rain,
and roses exploded
under his disciplined eyes,
he still couldn't claim
an Eden before the apple,
for one wild sunflower rose,
seeded unknown
in his boundaries of perfection,
cheating his guillotine of weeds,
reared her saffron head
and cried: Pick me,
and I'll sing you a song
of first love.

As the sunflower petals
teased through his fingers,
each falling
like small symmetrical suns
at his feet,   echoes
of childhood games:
I love you, I love you not.
I love you, I love you not.

The rim of soft fire
now almost undone,
the last petal throbbing
like a dark exotic woman
in his arms, softly breathing:

I am Eden, before, after, and now.

THE LION AND THE CROW

Still as stone,
crow lies anaesthetized
under God's gentle hands.
Gone the sheen of sun,
feathers now dull as lead.

Two angels
wearing blue masks
assist in the operation;
God opens the rib cage,
is in the chambers
of the heart.

"It's bloody and red,
I told you it's red," shouts God
into the accused lion's anxious face;
jungle eyes begin to squint,
mauling paws
go limp.

"Why, why did you do this?" asks God,
a curious but still angry look
in his eyes.
Lion coughs. "He was mouthy,
black and mouthy!
So I pawed him just once.

The arrogant little wimp
tried to fly away,
but I had the loafing wings
well pinned to scrub grass."

"You fool,
who lulls an ant to sleep
under an elephant's foot?

Certainly I made crow
bold, black and mouthy,
but also a shimmering shadow
against the sun.

And you   I made
king of the beasts,
though with some disabilities:
like getting your wife to hunt
for your meals, an attitude problem
and far too much siesta
under the acacia tree.

So, here's the solution:
you lion will keep
to the zebra and the wildebeest herds,
stroll the waterhole at dusk
like a king, roar
your mouth off as much as you desire,
but   hands off   crow!

I'll instruct
the foul-mouthed prince
to watch his language,
have him keep to simple domestic gossip,
and stop him from calling you names.

OK? Bullyboy?"

SUNDAY MORNING

Separate sounds,
church bells   bullets
intersect in the same man;
a black harbinger dog
limps across the Sunday sky.

The old wino's bottle
cries in its dregs,
alley walls soak in his pain,
wet stones
silently smudge a new grave,
and bodies in Sunday clothes
are slowly moving their limbs to pray.

The sun
without discrimination
warms the forgotten pulse,
the black smoking head,
Christ slumped against a garbage can,

and Sunday clothes
are slowly moving their bodies to pray.

THE UNEXPECTED HOUR

Breaking the Silence

He would sit there
and just look at you.
No thrusting eyes, nothing
unusual about his face,
his body a lump. It was as if
the mediocre flesh
was crowding your eyes like smoke.
But what really nipped at the heels,
drew blood,
smoked up his mother's heart,
was his silence,

a childhood kingdom
forged in some silent vocabulary,
a power unknown, unused;
words in his small mouth locked,
precious as gold, or,
snaked like cobra?

Then one day,
at God's unexpected hour,
he broke his silence
like a sudden rain,
and we like little children
crowded round
his merry-go-round of words,
some bitter and sweet as poetry

WHERE ADAM FIRST TOUCHED GOLD

Junction. The road forks
like a wishbone.
I choose neither, refuse
the destinies in separate highways.

And so I go for
the heart
of no man's land,
the immediate centre

that seems to belong
to no man and every man.

Here the division ends,
journey's anonymous oasis
where Adam shall continue
his fallen history.

Where the robin shall sing
with the voice of the paddy bird,
the oak wear the fruit of jak,
the crow soar with the eagle,

where the dreaming mind
shall have a choice
of coloured snows,
children play with old men,

and the sophisticated young
shall again learn their wisdom
from infants, their sanity
from grandfather fables.

I will not travel again
the separate paths of the sun,
the cruel geography of East and West
that blurs the mountain's blue mist,
the green valleys below.

Does it matter which way
the road turns,
there will always be another Grail,
another song, another weeping.

Wherever, the wind
will never let go its secrets.
Here, on undivided ground,
we'll fashion our own mythologies.

CONTAGION

Is this
>what they call
>the contagion of love?

After they held my feet
>to the palm-leaf fire,
>plucked the amulet
>of a dying God from round my neck,
>showed me
>how they flogged an old man
>in a sand pit;

after they spat on my face
>for preaching
>the saintly rhythms of the sun,
>how it slowly melts its empire
>into twilight and shadow, lets shadow
>fashion our nights of dream;

life, I said, should sing
>like the morning dove   end
>with the lullaby's sweet amnesia,
>not whine to the engine's smoking burn,
>falter and fall
>to the poison that bears no colour or smell.

So, tell me,
>what is the contagion of hate?
>What other masks, snarling faces,
>what new instruments
>will eke out the pain, fashion
>the last wet cough of death?

Will the wound
        continue to sing in its pus,
        will the spurting blood
        have no redemption?

Weathercocks are spinning
        in the wind,
        and we, the wise ones
        of cyberspace and moon journeys,
        we who sucked the cone
        in a hundred flavours,
        have now chosen to
        cut our paths
        into the dark unknown,
        and beyond!

"PASSION" WEEK

Only eight years old and I'm already convinced that Dad and Mum would sure make it to Heaven some day. For me, Dad's long hours with his Bible and black prayer book, Mum's daily recital of the rosary by the small altar in the corner of the living room, was enough evidence of their disciplined holiness. More. Nothing happened in the Crusz household without some reference to God, or Jesus, Our Lady, St Joseph or someone from the heavenly host of saints. How many times did I hear my father say that St Joseph was his favourite saint and was the patron saint of the family. Mother would sometimes conjure the fires of hell to persuade a stubborn child. When I broke in to say that Hilary would be an ideal candidate, I was promptly asked to shut up. So, obedience, daily mass (in my case as an altar server), Sunday mass, Sunday School were usual routines; rosaries, scapulars, holy pictures, prayer books were common artifacts about the house.

Passion Week turned out to be the hardest for us kids. Playtime cut in half, long night prayers on our knees (where we recited all the decades of the rosary); this was the week of no meat, no soda pop, no candy, no nightcap of Ovaltine; we were supposed to suffer with the suffering Christ. My brother Hilary, Mr Genius, Budding Scientist (as we gathered from rumours at school), took it hardest. He bucked and kicked like a stubborn horse at the home rituals for Passion Week. I, on the other hand, suffered in silence, determined not to taint the legend (according to my mother) of being the most obedient and delightful child of the tribe. Hilary and my other siblings countered, however, with such names as wimp, sissy, mamma's boy, snitch to characterize my more peaceful disposition.

Somewhere about the middle of Passion Week, Hilary grinds his teeth and goes creative: decides to present our own dramatic version of the Passion of Christ. I help to clean up the storeroom as venue, move Aunty Anne's heavy almirah, and put up a white bedsheet as curtain. Hilary had already carved a beautiful image of the crucified Christ from kadura wood, with the wounds of the Saviour prominently displayed with a generous splash of red ink. Dad was suitably impressed by Hilary's artistic skills; Mum immediately compares him to her elder brother who was a sculptor and architect. The idea of our passion drama was based on the Kawdana Players of Dehiwela, who sang the Jacomet Gonsalvez lamentations as they came to take down Christ from the cross.

Brother Vernon played the Roman soldier (who pierced the side of Christ); sisters Yvonne and Noeline were the women a the foot of the cross; brother Noel stood by as the beloved disciple, John. For audience, we had Aunty Daisy, Aunty Maud, Dad, Mum, Alice (the ayah), Soma (the cookwoman), Sirisena (the servant boy), and Bonzo the family dog. I had to strike a drum (an old kerosene tin) as Hilary chanted: "Father forgive them for they know not what they do." When my drumbeats turned erratic, Hilary in bated breath began swearing. Aunty Ada and Aunty Maud squirmed in their seats, and were about to rise when Mum stood up and gave Hilary her "fires of hell" look; Dad from left flank spewed a firm "DAMN!" The situation saved, THE CRUSZ PLAYERS brought the drama to a somber but successful end. Restrained applause, but a loud bark of approval from dog Bonzo!

FOREVER ADAM

Alone,
with only a fly   on the wall,
        naked,
but for a fig leaf,
        hunter
and hunted,

forever cuffed
        to jungle accoutrements:
a carnivorous tooth,
        for the intruder
that slips the raging moon,
        and dares
the waterhole of kings;

eye of the mongoose,
        razor teeth,
the way it tangos
        to the cobra's sway,
then strikes
        with the spasm of lightning;

eagle   wing span
        a long dark shadow
the killing beak, claws
        that can pluck
the prairie-dog
        like summer fruit.

Don't tell me.
        I know you're Adam
after the Apple,
        with now only a faint echo

of the tempter's voice
        about your ears,
as you balance and dance
        on this civilized edge.

But listen,
        I smell it.
I know it's there,
        hanging about the lobby,
sniffing entrances   exits,
        seeking
the red-carpeted stairs
        to your heart;

It has, of course,
        already been in and out
of your fool head,
        as if it were
the honoured guest
        of long ago.

TRAMP

After forty years,
this small cloister
holds the face of heaven
in its stone fists,
and Father Magee wears his tonsure
like a halo.

He now feels the thunder
of bread and water
gushing through his green veins,
can now call
to the brass Christ hanging
on the wall, and the Crucified One
will climb down to him.

Then the stigmata
from cold closing walls,
rituals of midnight prayer,
a leather whip singing
through his saintly bones.

Night.
And he sleeps on his wooden bed
with his God neatly folded
in his black cassock—
suddenly wakes   to a vision:
Francis feeding the birds
from the palm of his hand.

My God, cries Fr Magee,
are you really here,
in this cathedral of stone,
or basking outside with the birds
in the summer sun?

A tramp now walks
a thousand miles,
wraps yesterday's newspapers
against the icy winds,
sleeps with murders, wars and floods
round his cold skin;
babies, whores and policemen
dance like shadows in his dreams.

An old park bench
flings its arms open
to Frances Magee,
and a pigeon in a skullcap
of flaming feathers,
coos softly under his limbs.

Tonight,
Frances Magee bundles his God
in a cloak of hemp
and sleeps

in a cloister without walls.

FLIGHT OF THE WHITE BUTTERFLY

O Lord,   why?
why did you let her go
in immaculate wings   alone
into this last day of summer,
this field
that already sniffs
the coming of gusting thieves?

Where only the sun keeps
its red adolescence,
the buttercups sway
thinly pale, the lone pussywillow
droops with age,
and the fallen apples ferment
through their gnawed skins.

Where the grass
now curls in ruin,
and the distant elms hold on
to their moods,
silent and sentinel,
as if waiting
for the shame of nakedness.

Into this slipping audience,
you send her dancing,
tiny white ballerina
on a cushion of air,
minute bones all summer-oiled
for magnificent performance,
to contradict
these farewell moods, despair.

To boast
of the delicate lace round her body:
milk wings that riot
among the bleeding sumac;
to kiss the dandelions to blush,
doodle on the sky's absolute blue,
for the sun to catch
her white fire like diamonds.

To dance
her last act
to this tambourine of new wind,
to pirouette, cavort, gypsy
through the sunflowers,
arch to the dandelions' wine,
then leap again with the magic
of a prima donna's limbs.

O Lord,   why?
why when the sun
finally closed its red eyes,
did you let her go   alone
into the dark elms forever?
Did you prime her soft wings
to the catechism of a season,

to dance,
to die,
to end
this voluptuous summer?

RIENZI CRUSZ was born in Sri Lanka and came to Canada in 1965. Educated at the Universities of Ceylon, London (England), Toronto and Waterloo, he was for many years reference librarian at the University of Waterloo. He is now retired and lives in Waterloo. He has been widely published in magazines and anthologies in Canada and the United States. This is his tenth collection of poetry.

BOOKS BY RIENZI CRUSZ:

Flesh and Thorn
Elephant and Ice
Singing Against the Wind
A Time for Loving
Still Close to the Raven
The Rain Doesn't Know Me Any More
Beatitudes of Ice (TSAR Book)
Insurgent Rain (Collected Work, TSAR Book)
Lord of the Mountain (TSAR Book)
Gambolling With the Divine (TSAR Book)